a
mother

An Essandess
Special Edition
New York

We gratefully acknowledge the cooperation of the following schools: Hattie Martin Elementary School, Robstown, Texas; Mrs. O. B. Warner, Principal. □ Iona Grammar School, New Rochelle, N. Y.; Brother Martin P. Burns, C.F.C., Principal. □ King Street School, Port Chester, N. Y.; Mr. James Blancato, Principal. □ Park Avenue School, Port Chester, N. Y.; Mrs. Mary K. Bain, Principal. □ Scarborough School, Briarcliff Manor, N. Y., Grades 2, 3, and 4; Mrs. Dorothy Lawrence, Director of Lower School. □ Thornton-Donovan School, New Rochelle, N. Y.; Mr. Douglas Fleming, Jr., Headmaster. □ Windward School, White Plains, N. Y.; Mrs. Nan M. Shapiro, Dean of Admissions. □ Holy Trinity Elementary School, Mamaroneck, N. Y.; Sister Marie Raymond Henze, S.C., Principal.

WHAT IS A GRANDMOTHER

SBN: 671-10505-1

Granny comes to
your house about
3 times a year
but you go to her
house every Friday.

Heidi

a grandmother always
thinks you are going to
get hurt playing touch
football.

Dave

What my grandmother
mens to me
She is to cudel
you when you
have the mumphs

Maureen

A GRANDMOTHER
IS A PERSON
WHO LIKES TO
TEACH CHILDREN
WIERD MANNERS.

CHUCK

A Grandmother

My grandmother gives me candy or money. My other grandmother is just the same only she gives me meatballs or ice cream.

Kerry

My grandmother is a very old lady. Long long ago she was something like me.

Judy

Who is a grandmother

She is someone who tells mother
and father they're raising
me wrong.

Billy G.

A grandmother

is someone who can make
you fat and then love
you

by Laurence

Grandmothers

Grandmothers is
lusious lamb stew
or cream cupcakes
It's apple pie with
whipped cream or
chicken noodle soup
for me.

George

a grandmother
comes to football
games and cheers
when she doesn't
know whats
happening.

Rick

A grandma is made to
spoil you and save you
from your parents

Andy

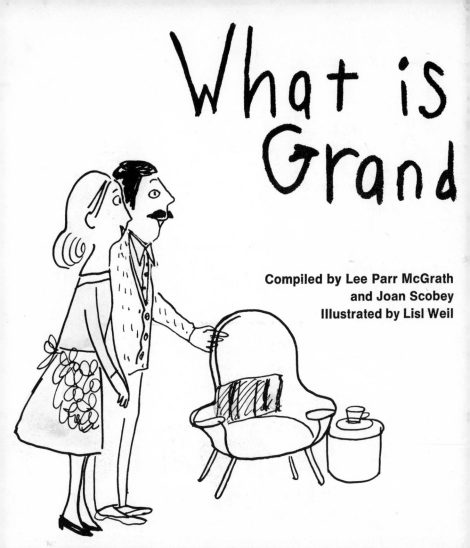

What is Grand

Compiled by Lee Parr McGrath
and Joan Scobey
Illustrated by Lisl Weil

to

from

What a Grandmother is

Whenever I go to see my grandmother and tell her not to fuss over lunch she goes ahead and does it. Well that's my grandmother for you.

Bruce

a grandmother will rush you to the hospital if you scratch your finger because she thinks you will die. They also are ser- usely disturbed about grems.

Eddie

a grandmother is that one
who gives you a Christmas
present your mother didn't
want you to have.

Bud

A grandmother is a second mother, or even better.

Mike

WHAT IS A GRAND MOTHER?
SOME ONE   WHO TELLS YOU
THE Bad THINGS YOUR MOTHER
DID WHEN SHE WAS A LITTLE
GIRL.

LOUISE

A grandmother is somebody
who visits and visits then
tells you she'll see you again soon

Kathy

Grandparents are people who spol you so much that your parent get grumpy

Drew

WHAT IS A GRANDMO-
THER?
WELL, I THINK A
GRANDMOTHER IS
SOMEONE WHO HAS TO
BE LOVED EVERY
MINUTE OF THE TIME
YOU GO THERE.

Janet

my grandmother is a groovy person. She rides a honda. She is married to a grandfather

Timmy

You can count on
A Grandmother to keep
you on the phone
while the one television
show you've been
waiting to seen is on.

Brian

Grandmothers play
with you whether they
are busy or not
That's why a grandmother
is my kind of person

Margaret

A grandmother is
always nice. You bring
them a boquet
of flowers and they
cry

Ricky

a grandmother is your
mother's mother and
your fathers mother too.

Julie

a grandmother
is not all up to
date.

Anne

What is a Grandma
She stays up and
wacthes the late, late,
late show then wakes
up at 6a.m.

How can she do
it?

Elizabeth

What is a grand-mother?

A grandmother is a lady with past experience.

Hughie

What is a grandmother?

She Can tell   Stories and
ferry tails 24 Hours a day, but
how I'm to big for grandmother
Stories

Jennifer

A grandmother is a person how spells the. way she talks.

Stevie

Granmothers do their
best to help out people.
They are also very
clean and reverent.

Bradley

a grandmother is
the one who stoffs
food down your
throat when you
are not Hungery

Billy

What is a grandmother?
When I send her a
letter she doesn't
just send back
another letter. She
puts something like a
dollor bill or a
hankerchef in
it   Patty

Grandmothers say
they have very
good memeriers
but they cant
remember how old
they are.

Tracy

There is nothing like
a grandmother: she
lets you put your
vegatables back in
the pot when your
mother isn't looking

Will

grandmothers buy you a dress that is too big for you this year. Then they say "Thats a nice length" dear.

Sharon

A grandmother is a nice old ladder. They worry and worry and worry. when thair nithing to worry about.

Susan

What is A Grandmother?
When my mother was
little she liked my
Grandmother.
Now I Sometimes Have
to protect my Grand-
mother
When my mother
Scolds Her.

Grace

Grandmother

ALL I CAN SAY IS THAT A
GRANDMOTHER LOVES YOU
A LOT BUT YOU HAVE TO
Be GOOD.

PETE

Who is a person
that gives you an
other jelly dough-
nut when your mother
says no? Your Grand-
mother!!!
Paul

GRANDMOTHERS
MY GRANDMOTHER GOES
HALLOWEENING WITH MY FRIENDS
AND ME. MY GRANDMOTHER IS
COOL.

THE END

JOHN

1934